CRUEL FICTION

COMMUNE EDITIONS

Red Epic, Joshua Clover
We Are Nothing and So Can You, Jasper Bernes
That Winter the Wolf Came, Juliana Spahr

A Series of Un/Natural/Disasters, Cheena Marie Lo
Still Dirty, David Lau
Maximum Ca'Canny the Sabotage Manuals, Ida Börjel

Blackout, Nanni Balestrini
Transnational Battle Field, ~~Heriberto Yépez~~
Special Subcommittee, Samuel Solomon

Excess—The Factory, Leslie Kaplan
Cruel Fiction, Wendy Trevino
Duppies, David Marriott

The Hammer, Adelaide Ivánova
Our Death, Sean Bonney

Cruel Fiction

WENDY TREVINO

Commune Editions
Oakland, California
communeeditions.com

An imprint of AK Press / AK Press UK
Oakland, California (akpress@akpress.org)
Edinburgh, Scotland (ak@akedin.demon.co.uk)

© 2018 Commune Editions
2nd edition 2019
3rd edition 2020
we encourage the sharing of this book and everything else: *omnia sunt communia*

Commune Editions design by Front Group Design
   (frontgroupdesign.com)

Library of Congress Cataloging-in-Publication Data

Wendy Trevino
   Cruel Fiction / Wendy Trevino
   ISBN 9781934639252 (pbk.: alk. paper)
   Library of Congress Control Number: 2018932448

Printed on acid-free paper by McNaughton & Gunn, Michigan, U.S.A. The paper
used in this publication meets the minimum requirements of ANSI/NISO Z39.48-1992
(R2009)(*Permanence of Paper*).

TABLE OF CONTENTS

128 - 131

From Santa Rita 128 - 131

[A LIST OF THINGS REMEMBERED AS I REMEMBERED THEM & IN NO WAY TO BE TAKEN AS A COMPLETE ACCOUNT OF WHAT HAPPENED THERE THEN OR WHAT IS HAPPENING THERE NOW]

I was detained approximately 54 hours, 47 of which I spent in jail.

I spent 47 hours under bright fluorescent lights.

I was cold approximately 43 hours.

I was moved 7 times, to 5 different "tanks."

I spent no more than 15 hours in a tank near a door with a small rectangle of glass through which 21 women & then 27 women could see barbed wire & light then dark outside.

I was fed 6 times—5 "sack lunches" which included 2 slices of stale bread, 2 slices of slimy bologna, 2 crème cookies soaked in bologna juice, 1 packet of "salad dressing" (mayo), 1 packet of mustard, 1 packet of a "calcium mix" & 1 orange; & 1 "hot meal," which included maybe turkey & definitely beans, a side of cooked carrots, some sauce, a salad, a cube of cornbread & a cube of cake.

I used a toilet no more than 5 times.

I slept no more than 4 hours.

I was denied birth control.

I heard someone with epilepsy was being denied medication.

I met 2 people with serious illnesses who were denied medication.

I watched 2 people go through withdrawal.

I watched 1 woman use 1 toilet at least 10 times in no more than 2 hours.

I spoke to 1 woman who confessed she was having suicidal thoughts.

I gave 1 back rub.

I received 0 back rubs.

I spoke to 3 people on "the outside."

I spoke to 3 "trustees."

I spooned 3 women.

I spooned 1 woman I had known previously.

I saw 2 women volunteer to stay inside longer to make sure 2 more women wouldn't be left alone in their respective tanks.

I saw 1 woman refuse release to make sure her friend would have a friend in the tank.

I met 1 woman with an "Abortions Get Babies to Heaven Faster" fanny pack she likes to wear when she visits Texas.

I saw 5 slices of bologna stick to a white wall.

I heard harmonizing coming from a tank 2 times.

I heard 1 person recite 1 poem to 2 pigs.

I heard I had 1 welt on my back.

I saw at least 5 bruises on each wrist.

I heard 1 woman suggest not admitting injury unless it was severe.

I met 2 women who chose not to report feeling ill for fear of being put in solitary confinement.

I met 1 woman who had been released from Santa Rita no more than 2 days before.

I crushed on 1 woman.

I was 1 of at least 5 women crushing on 1 woman.

I met at least 1 woman in a polyamorous relationship.

I met at least 1 woman who had recently had sex in the woods.

I met at least 1 woman who had recently had sex in a dressing room.

I met 1 woman who suggested we start a website to replace the #00 camp.

I met 3 women who were still in high school.

I had at least 5 pigs completely ignore me.

I heard at least 5 pigs lie at least 5 times.

I heard 1 pig compare the impact of the people the pigs had to process on "the system" to 400 marbles going down a drain 3 times.

I heard 1 woman praying.

I saw 1 appeal to "the Virgin" scratched into the wall of a tank.

I heard 2 women were put in solitary confinement.

I heard 1 woman was put in solitary confinement for scratching a word into the wall of a tank.

I saw "OCCUPY" scratched into the wall of a tank.

I heard 1 woman was placed in solitary confinement for banging on the door of a tank to get a pig's attention.

I saw at least 2 women kick the door of a tank at least 5 times in a row.

I saw 1 woman be forced into a tank.

I heard 1 pair of cuffs.

I heard 1 pig tell 1 woman if she had a problem with not getting a phone call she should call her lawyer.

I heard 1 pig say, "This isn't about the constitution…If I don't like your face…"

I heard 1 man banging on the door of his tank.

I heard 1 pig tell 1 trustee not to answer my question.

I met 2 women who requested that NLG contact their employers to let them know they would not be making it to work.

I met 2 women who were worried their arrest would lead to them losing their job.

I met 1 woman who lost her job as a union organizer when she was a "no show" after being arrested at a demonstration.

I met 1 woman who works as a union organizer.

I met 1 woman who works in San Francisco's Financial District.

I met 1 woman who can "crack" a house.

I met 1 woman with family in Spain.

I met 1 woman who teaches elementary.

I met 1 woman who said the games the pigs were playing with us were the same ones she plays with her kids.

I met 1 woman who teaches yoga.

I met 2 women who worried their car would be towed.

I met 1 woman who worried her boyfriend would forget to pay her parking ticket.

I met 1 woman whose boyfriend runs a comic book store.

I met 1 woman whose mother had bailed out Huey Newton.

I met at least 2 women who were afraid they wouldn't be able to get into a college class.

I met at least 3 women who were menstruating.

Bridesmaids came up 1 time.

I was 1 of at least 2 women who had seen *Bridesmaids*.

Kreayshawn's "Gucci Gucci" came up 1 time.

I heard 1 woman sing, "One big room / full of bad bitches."

Aquaman came up 1 time.

I saw at least 5 drops of fresh blood on the floor in the hall.

I saw at least 7 spots of dried blood on the wall of a tank.

I heard the riddle "What is brown & sticky?" 2 times.

I saw at least 15 wads of wet toilet paper stick to the air vents of 3 tanks.

I watched 4 women throw wads of wet toilet paper at the air vents of 3 tanks.

I heard 1 woman admit she was waiting to be released to take a "victory poop."

Kali came up at least 5 times.

"The 99%" came up 1 time.

I heard 1 pig call herself part of the 99%.

I heard 1 pig say the system had crashed, that we'd be inside at least 48 more hours, after we'd been detained 52.

I heard 1 pig threaten a mentally ill man.

I heard 1 pig make fun of a woman praying.

Dante's *Inferno* came up 1 time.

"Why am I being detained?" was chanted at least 10 ten times.

"Phone call!" was chanted at least 20 times.

"From Oakland to Greece, no pads no peace!" was chanted at least 10 times.

The Diva Cup came up 2 times.

I heard 1 woman call the inmates who worked at the jail "trustees."

I saw 13 people I'd previously met inside.

I saw 3 people without shoes.

I saw 2 people in "protective custody."

I saw 2 bologna faces.

Staying positive was equated with preparing for a class action lawsuit at least 3 times.

Poem

Santander Bank was smashed into!
I was getting nowhere with the novel & suddenly the
reader became the book & the book was burning
& you said it was reading
but reading hits you on the head
so it was really burning & the reader was
dead & I was happy for you & I had been
standing there awhile when I got your text
Santander Bank was smashed into!
there were barricades in London
there were riot girls drinking riot rosé
the party melted into the riot melted into the party
like fluid road blocks & gangs & temporary
autonomous zones & everyone & I
& we all stopped reading

Dude, You're an Asshole

*Everybody knows the centres of neutralisation, where it is required that no emotion
stands out, where each one has to contain himself & everybody experiences them
as such: enterprises (the family included), parties, sports centres, art galleries, etc.*

— *Call*, Tiqqun

You're a bumper, shock absorbers, brake pads
You're a scab, an officer in plain clothes, a plant with a sewing machine
You're the Christian indie rock band on the Kill Rock Stars label
You're the ambient mumbling of Interpol & attenuation
You know who you are
I am Keyser Söze, one of those women
Who hits back, I'm not interested in your metaphysics or discretion
Your inability to drive on the interstate or let your inner hyena out
I don't care if you can sympathize with the sentiment
                    Dude, you're an asshole
With your perfect playlist & spotless dance floor
With your simultaneous offerings of whisky, drinking etiquette & coffee
I refuse to dance at your lock-in or be ambushed
By your youth group, I refuse to call a dozen people wearing red
Awkwardly nursing their margaritas in a kitchen
A red party   I promise you will be negated
Fuck the Burning Man you read about

Poem

Don't believe everything you see on YouTube

    & I don't mean don't believe it

        The way you wouldn't believe something

On the cover of the *National Enquirer*; I mean

    Don't believe it like so many people

        Believed lonelygirl15. Don't place

Too much importance on a person's intentions

    Which for most people become clear

        Only with time. You know

There are so many videos that will show you

    How to do your hair like your favorite soap star.

        It's kind of incredible the innovations

That have been made in hair care products. Life

Before conditioner was never good

      & it didn't get better, but now when you get

Out of the shower it's easy to untangle your hair. It's not

     A metaphor or universal but the idea is your hair

       Will be soft

Again

FOR JOSH

I want to write an Alma who goes into the street.
With the sound of breaking glass all around you
She is close enough you hear the dead women
Out of nowhere say, "Take everything."

You are. A history of revolt resulting in new forms of oppression. You are concentrated in close proximity to the dilapidated plantations and ranches. You're at all the punk & hip hop shows. Something happened. The pigs went off. The jury came back with a verdict. Negotiations failed. The fascists were coming together. Comrades starving themselves in jail. You might have been skating less, which is how it is when what you do could at any point involve you in zip ties. Like leaving the house. If you have one. Whether you put it to yourself that way made no difference. You were done. Negative.

You think it'd be more interesting to write of being in it. To describe the dance, which is to say the steps. A barrage of arrivals & moving on. A constant refashioning of the on-hand. Almost midnight & you're saying Oakland, OK, I understand, comparing choices to all the protection you're supposed to have, "making them anyway"—to quote a friend.

Perez Hilton Link: That Heath Ledger Video:

I used to smoke 5 joints a day for 20 years: "Heath Ledger" [Heathcliff Andrew Ledger: the Clan Campbell, the Ledger Engineering Foundry, the Frank Ledger Charitable Trust [money: a bill rolled tightly: Heath Ledger on a mattress on a hard wood floor [East Austin, J, a razor blade on a guitar]: pharmaceuticals: SoHo: the SoHo Effect], Guildford Grammar School] at The Chateau Marmont [the Chateau: Sunset [Lake Austin, *I am big, etc.*, candy flipping], the Château d'Amboise [underground tunnels; Leonardo da Vinci; Mary, Queen of Scots; the Amboise conspiracy; bodies strung over the railings of the Gothic wing], hotel & bungalows [John Belushi naked in NO. 3: speedballs/moonrocks [Project MKULTRA: Dr. Frank Olson]: Mitch Hedberg [paraprosdokian [J, broken furniture on a lawn], non sequitur, red cups] in New Jersey: River Phoenix outside the Viper Room [River Jude Bottom: Children of God/the Family International: evangelism: flirty fishing: Ricky Rodriguez: The Story of Davidito]: Chris Farley on a billboard], seismic retrofitting], 26, loaded, etc.

Summer 2016

FOR ANTIFA SACRAMENTO & THOSE YOUNG PEOPLE IN SAN JOSE WHO BEAT THE BEJEEZUS OUT OF TRUMP SUPPORTERS

It's 11:30 in San Francisco. Britain has voted
To leave the EU. Last week, the Golden
State Warriors lost to the Cleveland Cavaliers
In the NBA Finals. We watched the game
On a flat–screen TV set up outside a bookstore
In Downtown Oakland. Right next to a vegetarian
Chinese restaurant that had been shot up
During a vigil the week before. Josh wanted
Cleveland to win. Mostly for Tamir Rice.
Mostly hoping Black people in Cleveland would
Finally get their riot. I want that, too.

This is the week after I turn 38 & 49
Gay & queer men & women—Black & nonblack
Latinx, nearly half Puerto Rican—are killed
In a mass shooting at a gay night club
In Orlando. Right down the street
From where the contestant of a popular reality
Television show had been shot & killed by her stalker
The night before. Not too far from a Disney resort
Where 5 alligators are captured & gutted
By authorities looking for the remains
Of a 2-year-old boy who is dragged

By an alligator into a lake a couple of days later.
This is the same month a gorilla born & raised

Where I was—in the Rio Grande Valley
Of South Texas—is killed at the Cleveland Zoo
After he drags a toddler who falls into his exhibit
Around. Later that week, Jane Goodall calls
The zoo to say it looked like the gorilla was
Was trying to protect the kid. I don't know.
This is weeks before white nationalists
With the Traditionalist Workers Party stab antiracists
Who stop them from holding a rally in Sacramento.

Before a frightening number of people argue
That the rights of the white nationalists were
Violated like that's a bad thing. This is after
A crowd of mostly teenagers—mostly nonwhite—
Chase supporters of Donald Trump's presidential
Campaign out of San Jose. After someone takes
A picture of a white kid running frantically away
From a group of nonwhite kids running after him.
This is the same month it's announced
Puerto Rico's water will no longer be monitored
For quality, because having defaulted on its debt

The country can't afford it. After the murder of 2
Activists who exposed the contamination of Flint
Michigan's water supply. After militia men "open-carry"
As they deliver bottled water to Flint residents.
& I'm writing from the future, where all over
The United States Black people are blocking highways
& carrying guns to protests where the cops can see them.
This is the week cell phone videos of 2 Black men
Being murdered by cops go viral on consecutive days.
Before Micah X. Johnson kills 5 cops in Dallas
During a Black Lives Matter march. This is a couple

Of weeks after teachers block highways in Oaxaca
& an anarchist is arrested & run over by cops. & I keep
Thinking I will call this "11:30" because that's the time
I started writing one night a month ago & it's
Something I'll come back to—more like a workday
Than a ray of light through a cloud. I guess that's

What feels different—like highways full of people
There's no way around & barricades & teenagers setting
Cop cars on fire. It's inevitable. Maybe we'll see each other.

5 Out of 13 Ways of Looking at Poetry Not Being Enough

1.
If you were to wear a shirt that said LEAVE ME ALONE
People might not talk to you or harass you or assault you.
You might put them off. You might manage
To trick them, this time. That you weren't even trying
Is a terrible sign—like an intersection with signs
That say DON'T STOP KEEP GOING.

2.
It's the difference between ALL ROADS LEAD
TO THE KILL FLOOR & YOU CAN SEE
YOURSELF OUT. I'm talking about the promises
Of art & the promises of civil war. I'm saying the coldness
Of that adjective is no match for the heat in parts of the south
Or for being without water or running out of food.

3.
People make things that reflect how they live, where.
These things are not to be confused with the shadows
They cast. When I write a poem I write about things
Like shadows, execute certain tricks. I can see why
People have compared it to dance, but have you ever
Danced in the streets? It's better not to do it by yourself.

4.
Terrorist attacks are a consequence of wars
You're not supposed to know about. Planes
Flying into towers don't start wars more than you
Not shopping. It's no wonder you believe magicians are men
With magic hats that double as wormholes for rabbits
From galaxies far far away & magical women for so long.

5.
At most, I can see a painting being like a bluff, a view
Of the back of your opponent's cards when you're playing
For money & you've already lost more than you planned.
But your relationship with it isn't the most important
Or interesting one. Your love won't change what a painting
Is, which is someone's time spent working for someone else.

Phalanstery for Imaginary Friends

In fact, young children are very dialectical; they see everything in motion, in
contradictions and transformations

— *A Companion to Marx's Capital*, David Harvey

Bloo was like a hippy telling a Buddhist to shut up
Because he wouldn't stop telling people to shut up
Because throughout the war they'd been so

Quiet Eduardo was like César Chávez & Che shaking their heads
Like Pinky mirrors Firefly in *Duck Soup* like who wore it better
Frames dresses & action figures the last that nobody

Comes in Wilt lost like most of his arm was imagined tall
Father stay at home like a Coca Cola-iced tea taste test
Grandma sister's husband's brother &

Still alive Coco could do slapstick but only at podium like Harpo
Like that was a curse contingent with credit the university's call
For jihad against the Cotillion PTA the criminalizing of

Slapping Mr. Herriman fought in one of the wars worried he enjoyed
Shopping for his girls too much sent them all to college
But was mostly tired always between meetings a

Communist Cheese was post-*Dr. Strangelove* pre-something id-shaped smudge
Spread around the eyes of Jackie Kennedy in the commonest
Of dreams the passports & degrees counterfeit

Poem

then you're there & you're unpaid, the city's there, beautiful
like anyone stepping off the sidewalk as somewhere
to something is added a star where a lifetime might pass

peaceful fascists & riot police work together
the video goes viral, not so much to convince, but for history
nothing personal

then the refrain: "normalcy reigns.
no one predicts anything out of the ordinary.
horoscopes call for more of the same." a sober man ponders a missile

then its self-portrait &
you're beautiful
but it's not that either

a sustained unconscious function or "analyze this"
with quotations like wings for the suburbs, lots of intimate time with the radio
fair enough

Trampa De Dedos / Finger Trap

AFTER RAQUEL SALAS-RIVERA

Should

you

put a ring on it

spiral out, forget

this is another becoming

you turn in, like Lucille Clifton "turning into [her]

own / turning on in / to [her] own self / at last / turning out of the / white cage, turning out

of the / lady cage / turning at last." A person born with twelve fingers isn't a metaphor for anything, but if you would like her to

she'll read your palm. When you meet her, that's what she says. It's 2008. Not too long before the stock market crash. At a poetry retreat in an offensively named town where timeshare people go to ski & dream about Aspen.

Around this time, you love Charles Simic's translation of Vasko Popa's sequence "The Little Box" more than just about any other book of poems. The little box can be anywhere & nowhere. You can store & lose the entire world inside her as the little box falls in love with herself & conceives a little box that falls in love with herself & conceives…

Infinite little boxes! You maintain that sequence is good, but in retrospect, your love of the little box seems like a compromise. So many young poets you meet between 2004 & 2008 have been influenced by Michael Hamburger's translations of poems by Paul Celan, but you can't read those beautiful translations without remembering what the poet Joe Wenderoth said about Celan's suicide note to his wife. All it said was her name & "all light." It may be written in French. The historical context of Celan's poems—you can't stop thinking about that.

At the same time, a significant number of young writers—many of them teenage girls—are chatting online with Tao Lin or some other depressed man in his early 20s. They call this "Alt-Lit." This is before one Alt-Lit woman turns up in an anarchist space in San Francisco & starts sleeping with one of the editors of a communist journal called *Endnotes* but after Kenneth Goldsmith "transcribes" the September 11, 2001 issue of the *New York Times*. publishes *The Day* & writes about being the most boring writer that ever lived. At the same time, more & more young artists & writers move to East Austin. It is recommended that you spend a few good years teaching English in Korea or Japan. Hundreds of thousands of Iraqi civilians are killed by the United States. If talking about the past historically doesn't mean recognizing it "the way it really was," to what extent does it involve something like translation?

Does translation require a person or just language anymore? What is the legal age of consent in New Jersey & New York? These, perhaps, were some of the big questions some people were asking. "Providing scientific articles to those at elite universities in the First World, but not to children in the Global South?"—that was another. Aaron Swartz left Reddit. Open access is nothing like an exhibit at a museum. It's not even like a museum membership. Not even like a highway shut down. The tech buses have been around longer than many people think. Fukuyama had predicted an obsession with form removed from anything like political life, as if the hipsters of the mid-aughts would invent nihilism. Some poets begin to speak in terms of a sincerity / irony binary. It's possible the binary doesn't apply to anything of note—not even in the always late United States where young people in black fuck up Starbucks & the Gap during the 1999 WTO protests in Seattle. Then again some of them claim a swastika can be ironic, while others claim it's merely cultural, which is to say marginalized people should calm down, which is to suggest a swastika is a swastika is a swastika, which is to say it's the swastika you're afraid of, what the swastika can do & not the history of the people who make it what it is, which is not over, which is dead wrong.

The We of a Position

I started writing this at 6 this morning, after 5 hours of sleep, after a night of doing nothing, after a couple of hours talking on the phone with Lauren Levin, after a day of seeing a very disorganized friend off to Kuwait, where he will teach for two years in order to have a free place to live & pay off a fraction of his grad student loans.

I started to make a list of things that have happened, beginning with "global financial crisis" & ending with me standing here in Oakland, reading something about labor, writing & fighting. Without even trying to include everything, I ran out of steam by the time I got to the third instance of "looking for work" & the first word of students occupying UC buildings.

I started to respond to a piece that Stephanie Young so generously sent me, a piece that included a piece of something I'd said about working with people that are hard to work with, people you might not like all that much or at all, people you might not know. How it is still possible, how it is already how most people work every day in jobs they wish they didn't need. How it reminds me of my family, a very large group of people that includes people who just appeared in a field to work one day. How it isn't a family in the traditional sense. How it includes a kid named Taco, an orphan who would ask for tacos from other field hands, a kid the barrio my mother grew up in took in. How it includes a woman my mother met working in the fields & her son & another woman who took care of me as a child. How it includes the neighbors my mother lived with when she ran away from home at thirteen as much as an undocumented worker my mother recently met on a flight to New York. How the support these people have given each other is financial as well as emotional. How in continuing to support each other some of these people risk losing their jobs. Some of them risk worse.

I started to think about my father picking cotton as a kid & the hierarchy of the fields. How poor whites & Mexican-Americans got first pick. How undocumented workers went in second & African-Americans picked last. How my father said getting first-pick made him feel special until one very hot day, in Lubbock, during a break, his family went looking for water. How none of the white people in town would give them water. How on their way back to the fields, a truck of African-American farm hands offered them some. How they didn't even have to ask. How my father says we're all living like that—not even knowing who our friends are. How my father passes for white until he speaks. How a farmer & his wife, in College Station, told my grandmother they would adopt my father & raise him as white when he was four years old. How the men who hired my father at AT&T in the seventies laughed & said they were meeting the requirements of affirmative action with a man who "talks like a Mexican but looks white." How, when my father tells this story, he doesn't even seem mad.

I started to worry that what I was writing was dealing too much with identity without dealing with it. I remembered why I hesitate to talk about these things. Because what I am trying to say is that we should really think about who our friends are. What I am trying to describe is what is described in Tiqqun's *Call* as "the we of a position." A "we" that includes people we do & don't like. A "we" that includes people we haven't met yet & people we will never meet. A "we" that sees the hierarchy of the fields & calls bullshit without being dismissive of its bullshit effects. A "we" that is aware of other fields.

I started to worry that I would cry reading this in front of a room full of people I respect & am just getting to know. Mostly because I read what I'd written to Dereck, my partner & he said some of you might cry. I started to consider having Dereck read this & worried about the effect a white man, an adjunct professor from a working class family might have on the text. A white man whose grandfather grew up on a Choctaw reservation, moved to Arkansas & bought land because it had once been illegal for Native Americans to cross the Oklahoma border into certain parts of Arkansas. I wondered which option I would worry about, then do anyway.

I wanted to talk about how I started slowly to see this "we." How I had been looking for work, then working six days a week & all that time reading. Reading Sianne Ngai's *Ugly Feelings*, thinking about envy, asking, "To what extent do homosocial group formations rely on antagonism?" Reading Ian Baucom's *Specters of the Atlantic: Finance Capital, Slavery & the Philosophy of History*, thinking about the British slave ship *Zong*. Reading the first chapter of Marx's *Capital* for the nth time, listening to David Harvey's podcasts. Reading Foucault's *Discipline & Punish*, engaging in an argument about Social Networking Sites, weak intimacy & collective action in because poetry is not enough, a "secret" group on facebook consisting of me, Brian Ang, Tiffany Denman, Joseph Atkins, Jeanine Webb, May Ought, Erin Steinke & Dereck Clemons. In a cubicle, an unpaid intern, arguing on Facebook, with people I do & people I do not often see, arguing "I'm not sure the weak intimacy that characterizes even strictly fb relationships is so different than that of the intimacy characterizing most work relationships or relationships between peers & while it is true that relationships are implicit in collectivizing & while propinquity remains a determining factor in whether one participates in a particular collective action, I think it's a mistake to think people have to be on intimate terms with each other prior to collectivizing / in order to collectivize."

Revolutionary Letter

one thing i've learned / come to a provisional conclusion about:
when it comes to fighting, there are people who will help you
fight & there are people who will not & there are people
who will stand in the way. find the people who will help / be loud
& clear so they know where you are — focus on them, be encouraged
by them, encourage them, work with them. don't worry
about the people who won't help. they will be of no help even
if they are on your side. waste as little energy as possible
fighting people who stand in the way, which is to say don't talk
don't argue, just get them out of the way of the fight you came for.

tl;dr: you don't need or want
the people who you know
aren't "with you" to be
with you. really, you don't

POPULAR CULTURE & CRUEL WORK

AND I JUST WANT YOU
TO KNOW THAT THIS ISN'T ME,
BEING INTERESTED IN THESE
THINGS, BUT ME, BEING
INTERESTED IN YOUR BEING
INTERESTED IN THESE THINGS

— UYEN HUA

IN MOMENTS OF EXTREME PAIN, I'VE SCRATCHED
THE EDGES OF MYSELF, HOPING TO DELINEATE A
MEANING, A SHAPE, THE SHORES OF AN OCEAN,
WHICH MAY BE EVERYWHERE & ROUGH BUT EXIST[S].
BUT IT SEEMS IMPORTANT TO DO THAT TOO WHEN
I'M NOT SUFFERING SO MUCH & FIND HOW & WHERE
[ARE] THE SHORES OF FRIENDSHIP.

— OKI SOGUMI

1.

"No matter how much you feel it, you want
To feel it even more." That's the feeling
Tony Bennett says he sees in Amy
Winehouse when they meet to record "Body
& Soul" in March 2011
For Bennett's album *Duets II*. All this
For an "honest recording." She'll be gone
By August. The album will debut at
No. 1 in September. Her parents
Will accept a Grammy on her behalf
In February 2012. "What
Can I say," her father will say, "Long live
Whitney Houston! Long live Amy Winehouse!
Long live Etta James!" But they'll all be dead.

2.

What the entertainment industry learned
From Buddy Holly, in the days after
The music died, is that there are few things
More lucrative than the untimely death
Of a rising star. & in the case of
Selena, Queen of Tejano, there was
Even more to be made off images
Of collective mourning, as "Latinx"
Coalesced into a new market that
Became part of the story. Howard Stern
Played the xenophobic American
For the shock value, while in Mexico
1,000,000 people lost their jobs & the
Feminicides in Juárez didn't stop.

3.

When JonBenét Ramsey's father starts
Dating Natalee Holloway's mother
You can't tell if it's art or life being
Imitated or by what. The truth is
Burying a middle-class white girl is
A lot cheaper than paying someone to
Explain her body. Anyway, you'd be
Surprised what can stimulate tourism.
Like Anna Nicole Smith in a graveyard
In the Bahamas buried next to her
Son. You go to bed thinking about this
All the time — about the girls whose deaths bring
People together. You made them famous.

4.

When John Singleton is interviewed in
The middle of the LA Riots, he
Says Mike Tyson wasn't convicted by
A jury of his peers. He says a Black
Man can go to jail for kicking a dog
While Soon Ja Du is given probation
For killing Latasha Harlins. Rodney
King is who most people associate
With this time, but the riots are about
More. Tupac autographed looted copies
Of his CD & a week later said
"I told you so." Latino men between
18 & 24 accounted for
30% of people arrested.

5.

Tuco joins the Sinaloa Cartel
Kills Blondie & there's no epic final
Duel, no Angel Eyes. The invisible
Hand of the black market makes it hard to
Tell where all that Confederate gold goes.
This is *The Good, the Bad & the Ugly*
In *No Country for Old Men*. Sheriff
Ed Bell is depressed & hit man Anton
Chigurh is art imitating the life
Of Woody Harrelson's dead dad.
Did drug cartels kill the Western or pay it to
Look the other way? Did drug trafficking
Save the banks during the 2008
Global financial crisis? Seriously.

6.

What if popular culture is no more
Than me being interested in your
Being interested in these things that
You're interested in my being
Interested in—except you & me
Are interchangeable & so many
& making things interesting enough
That capitalists pay each other to
Sell us back these things? What if it's music
That's behind the music & we are just
Walking around with that Cranberries song
Stuck in our heads? Mostly, I have questions
& don't want to find myself. I'd rather
Look at my choices & yours. Yup. Nope. Yup.

7.

FOR BG

"This was not a somber event; this was
One of Los Angeles's largest parties."
This was OJ's last run. This was a white
Ford Bronco going 35 miles
Per hour on Interstate 405.
People stopped their cars & got out to watch.
"The conditions are always there." Thousands
Might up & block a highway or riot
In front of a "suspect's" house just to stop
An arrest. On June 17, 19-
94, you could see that happening.
The 95,000,000 Americans
Watching it all unfold on TV could
See that happening. A lot of us did.

8.

You might have to be driving in Texas
Under a wide blue sky with a hard white
Cloud here & there to actually hear Tom
Petty. There might need to be something you're
Done with. You might want to finally be
Ready to see where your life is going
& brave enough to go through it.
You might try admitting you were wrong: you don't grow
Out of good music. You become aware
Of another you not just surviving
But becoming still more distinct & hard
To read. It gets hard to say if that's you
In the past or future. Tom Petty sings
"The future was wide open" & that helps.
.

9.

*Aboard the Planet of the Apes About
The Planet of the Apes According to
The Planet of the Apes Across from the
Planet of the Apes Across the Planet
Of the Apes After the Planet of the
Apes Against the Planet of the Apes Out
Of the Planet of the Apes Outside the
Planet of the Apes Over the Planet
Of the Apes Owing to the Planet of
The Apes Past the Planet of the Apes As
Of the Planet of the Apes Atop the
Planet of the Apes Barring the Planet
Of the Apes Because of the Planet of
The Apes Before the Planet of the Apes*

10.

I was in a vintage clothing store on
Valencia called Shauplatz when I found
Out Michael Jackson had died. I started
Crying. "Oh, Honey, don't cry. Prince is still
Alive," one of the men who ran the store
Said. From my apartment on 25th
Street, you could hear cars honking & blasting
"Beat It" until it got dark. It was like
When El Salvador beat Mexico in
A World Cup qualifier days later
Or when the Giants won the World Series
The next year, except "we" felt bigger while
Sharing this loss. Josh says he thought it would
Go down, which is more or less what I mean.

.

11.

FOR THE JIVE YOUNG KINGS

What killed Prince likely also killed Pittsburgh
Folk hero Danny Montano less than
A month after he was acquitted on
39 counts of vandalism. He
Wrote AESIA, BROWN EYES, SPACE BOY & MF
ONE — MF as in Mad Fresh, Moonlight Fiend
& Motherfucker. That halo that forms
Around the moon before bad weather comes
He called "the circle of protection." He
Was invisible to cops when he wrote
In that light. They could only see he'd been
There once he'd gone. The "artists" interviewed
In *Style Wars* were wrong. Some writers don't
Just want space to write. They want everything.
.

.

12.

The question is what celebrity will
Come out in support of antifa next?
Maybe the Kanye who looked straight into
The camera during a live benefit
Concert for the victims of Hurricane
Katrina on NBC & said "George
Bush doesn't care about Black people" to
8.5 million viewers will come back.
It's been more than a decade of watching
That clip & laughing at the look on Mike
Myers's face & waiting for Kanye
To say something that people elsewhere are
Screaming again, not because it will fix
Anything but because why not / he can.

13.

In the last year of the millennium
Subcomandante Marcos recorded
A message to Rage Against the Machine
& Tijuana NO! expressing his
Admiration & addressing the bands'
Relevance, not only to the struggle
Of Zapatismo, but to student strikes
At UNAM in Mexico City, where
The bands later played the recording for
Fans who'd come to the Palacio de
Los Deportes to see them in concert.
The same year: 400 cops protested
Rage Against the Machine outside a show
In Massachusetts. The band sent donuts.

14.

JClo says what "rage most wants is context.
Otherwise it destroys you." I agree.
More importantly, what he says helps me
Think about this bad feeling I tend to
Get when I explain what I do in terms
Of popular culture—maybe it's just
Culture. It's recursive & fucking fun.
I want to be able to just enjoy
It. Then I realize I've just referenced
A protest song that is clearly against
Violence & in a way that doesn't make
Clear that I'm not against violence & that
I don't have much to say about protest
Songs or write them & that needs to be clear.

15.

If I am being completely honest
Joni Mitchell confuses me. She looks
Like someone who would annoy me & her
Music seems like music I wouldn't be
Into. On the other hand, she doesn't
Annoy me & I'm into her music.
The friends who introduced me to *Blue* in
The 90s left *Ladies of the Canyon*
In my car & none of us brought it up
For a long time. Her voice reminds me of
Space travel & sirens; man landing on
The moon & Odysseus bound tight to
A mast, sailing away. I forget she's
From Canada & not California.

16.

FOR MONICA TREVIÑO

Selena had already "crossed over"—
From the regional Tejano music
Market into the multinational
Latin music market—with her breakthrough
Album *Entre a Mi Mundo* & it's
Less that more Latinos had come around
To Tejano & more that her band's core
Members hadn't been fans of the music
Either. They'd blown Mexico's huge Latin
Music audience away with their funk
Reggae & pop influenced approach to
The Afro-Columbian cumbia
"& once you break into Mexico, that
Tidal wave is felt in California."

17.

FOR JOSH & EDDIE

It's not that I want to bring Chicano
Nationalism back. The supposed
Historical basis for Chicano
Identity involves the erasure
Of Black Mexicans & obscures the fact
That indigenous peoples still make up
More than 20% of Mexico's
Population. Besides, of what use is
That identity to a movement that
Isn't about us & against borders?
Still, I don't want cholos & cholas to
Disappear & I'm not just hanging on
To a style that at this point almost
Anyone can have. I want everything.

18.

FOR XARI & EDGARDO

If Selena stood for the cultural
Promise of NAFTA, that might explain why
"Read NAFTA papers" & "Strategize plan
For Mexico" are the 4th & 5th things
On one of her last lists of to-dos. It
Explains the notable silence around
Zapatismo. The promise would've been
To Americans, including those "ni
De aqui ni de alla" who were still
Model citizens of the United
States. She would've had her own free market
Fantasies about "the American
Dream" & how she was going to live it
& not ever forget where she came from.

19.

FOR CHINGA LA MIGRA

If a woman illegally crossing
The US-Mexico border can sing
The Border Patrol agent's favorite
Selena song, will he still detain her?
What if he does & later writes about
Her in the patrol vehicle's back seat
Singing his favorite Selena song?
Will the Selena fans who read his book
Like it? What if that scene in *Reservoir
Dogs* where Mr. Blonde tortures a cop had
Been choreographed to "Bidi Bidi
Bom Bom," instead of "Stuck in the Middle
With You?" Would the Border Patrol agent
Be more or less likely to like that scene?

20.

It's hard to care about what the rich do
To hurt themselves. It's hard not to root for
Whatever they're on to do them in while
They lose their kids in a dream. What about
The people who aren't dreaming? Who always
Feel like they are, like all they want is to
Wake up because then sleep is possible.
Lately, we've been spending a lot of time
Together. The wider the gap between
Us the more time we spend, especially
Now that they're coming back to the cities.
I moved to the most beautiful city
I had seen as a kid to get out of
A government job. So here we are. Sweet.

21.

I keep trying to see what you all see
In Anzaldúa. You want your theory
To be fleshy, even if its flesh feeds
Off the flesh of struggling indigenous
People. You can't describe the cruel fiction
Race is without history, which did not
End. Indigenous people are still in
It. Black Latinx are still in it. Maybe it's
Because capitalism treats us so
Interchangeably that we forget we
Are who we are & what we do with each
Other. If who you are depends on you
Ignoring the Zapatistas, who are
You becoming? Who will you say you are?

22.

When I think about what it means to be
A feminist, I think about being
A bad feminist. About how I've been
One. About how I wrote my ex-husband's
English papers in college. About how
I filled out his grad school applications.
About how I didn't do any of it
Selflessly. About how I wanted more
Than anything to get out of Texas.
About how much easier I thought that
Would be if my boyfriend got into school
Out of state. About how I was convinced
I needed him, if I was going to
Leave my family. Like I couldn't just move.

23.

Carlos Ferrer's maid. At an expensive
Private college in Central Texas, that's
Who I thought I was. How I saw myself
In relation to the people I was
Around. I was the kind of girl guys like
Che Guevara want to play with. & by
"Guys like Che," I mean guys from money, not
Revolutionaries. That's the feeling
That, at page 9, was so strong I had to
Put his bio down. I was right to stop
Playing. It wasn't just a feeling, but
Looking at that passage, I also see
The self-absorption & myopia
I'm capable of. I'll come back to that.

24.

Heartbreak is a march gone terribly wrong.
You don't want to have to go into work
The next day. You don't want to be inside
At a computer where no one can help
You. Where you can't even help yourself.
"It's a career," my boss says. She hates that
I call it "a job." I write about work
Since there's no escaping it. Like heartbreak.
Work structures so much life. According
To Human Resources, I'm white. I have
Been confused for other women with dark
Hair. Maybe I am them sometimes. In the
Elevator, taking the stairs, walking
Back from lunch, insisting "this isn't me."

25.

I remember one of my professors
In grad school—the only woman who taught
Poetry in the program. She once expressed
Disappointment with my poems. She said
I must have experienced interesting
Things as a "Mexican woman"—she wished
She could see that in my poems. I know this
Isn't what she meant, but maybe one day
She'll read these sonnets & know what she said
Stuck with me. I remember the one time
I called my mom a feminist. She got
Mad. Defensively, she said, "No, I'm not."
I don't know all her associations
With that word, but now I can imagine.

26.

FOR BROOKE

It's September 9, 2016.
I'm not sure why I've been so reluctant
To keep going. I keep starting over
Somewhere else & I keep reading. I'd like
To do more than tell "stories everyone
Likes to pretend they don't know." Anyway
The stories most important to me aren't
Stories I can share, with more at stake than
Who speaks at a conference. What came out of
Taking risks together has, at one time
Or another, damn near shattered the heart
Of every person I got to know. We
Weren't taking the same risks. That's the moral
Of every story. That's why I'm still here.

27.

The first time boys in Che's social mileu
Had sex it was usually "an Indian
Or poor mestiza" servant girl they had
Sex with, but looking again at the part
Of Che's bio where Ferrer & his friends
Spy on Che having sex with Ferrer's maid—
"La Negra" Cabrera—I noticed what
They called her, the easy racism of
Comfortable boys. I was never Ferrer's
Maid. I don't even know where she was from.
She should have her own narrative like
One of Saidiya Hartman's wayward girls.
& the history of slavery & white
Men & Black women—that'd be part of it.

28.

AFTER & FOR JAMIE BERROUT

The word "disposable" keeps coming up.
The "disposable female bodies" of
Women in Juarez. The "disposable
Domestics" & low-wage workers that First
World structural adjustment policies
Imposed on the Third World helped to create.
Or I'll read a description that all but
Uses the word. The (Black) girls involved in
Sex work whose schools are "throwing them away."
The "women (trans, disabled, Black & brown
Sex workers) [seen] as marked for destruction
…society sees…as natural, even
Necessary." I haven't stopped trying
With feminism—or, at least, women.

29.

Capitalism is bad for women —
Be they cis or trans. Whoever we are
We start there. Not all women will agree.
Let's be honest: the brutality
Of capitalism's not as brutal
To some women. For instance, in Juárez
Not every woman's body is seen as
"Disposable." The women whose bodies
Rosa-Linda Fregoso refers to
Are racialized, as well as gendered &
Poor. Can we admit what it means to be
A woman — what it requires you do
Daily depends on other things you are?
& you have to hate capitalism.

30.

FOR THE 57,000 & 2.3 MILLION #ALLOFUSORNONEOFUS

The largest prison strike in the history
Of the US is still going. "We want
[You] to understand the economics
Of the prison system…It's not about
Crime & punishment. It's about money,"
Inmate & organizer Melvin Brooks-
Ray says. Whoever we are we're also
Against the state, prisons & cops. Against
The enforcement of gender. Confinement.
We know the war has to be total. It's
Just like that. We're against borders & choose
Who we want around us. I think it will
Get harder. We can't forget Diana
La Vengadora. It might come to that.

BRAZILIAN IS NOT A RACE

1.

& I'm not sure how important that is
When you're from Ukraine. I don't give a fuck
What Elizabeth Bishop said. Never
Did. You can like her I'm just saying I
Don't care what she had to say about race.
I will not center some racist settler
Woman's mistaken ideas about
The world in order to make love & hate
Less complicated. Why destroying what
Destroys you is more difficult than you
Expect every time: that complication.
Which is to say I'm not sorry: Clarice
Lispector was white, that passage sounded
Anti-black & that's not "fucked up" to say.

2.

When I said race is relational what
I meant is people are racialized in
Relation to other people who have
Power. It isn't enough to not like
Mexicans. Where I'm from, many of us
Mexican-Americans resented
The Mexicans who came to South Texas
To shop for designer clothes. They were rude
& treated at least the working class &
Poor & undocumented Mexican-
Americans as bad as the "Anglos,"
Which is what we called the white people, who
May or may not have hated Mexicans
Who worked with a few of them anyway.

3.

I took dance classes with two Mexican
Girls. They went to private school in Brownsville.
I remember thinking one of them was
Very pretty. I remember seeing
Them shopping in the mall once & my mom
Pointing out how they were shopping alone
With their parents' credit card & she watched
With what seemed like awe as the pretty one
Paid for an expensive GUESS jean jacket
& complimented her taste. My cousins—
Some of them—were Mexican too. I thought
I was whatever they were. Those teenage
Girls shopping with their parents' credit card
Were definitely from Mexico though.

4.

A childhood friend was visiting while
I wrote this poem. I tried to explain what
I'm talking about here to him & said
"Like Beth Singerman & Ruth Kohn [kids
From middle school] were Argentinian."
"They were?" he asked. "Yeah & they were also
White, which is why they hung out with the white
People & why you thought they were just your
Run-of-the-mill white people," I said. It
Might have been the case that some of their white
Friends didn't think they were white enough, since
They were Jewish or not US born. Can't
Say for sure. We weren't close for very long.
They split us up in high school, like they do.

5.

My childhood friend who was visiting
While I wrote this poem, had visited our
Hometown by the time he met up with me
In San Francisco. He said it had changed.
He said that since Hurricane Katrina
Harlingen's Black population had grown.
He said, "Thank God." I told him that only
Recently had I realized that some of
Us were Afro-Latino. Actually
I said I had realized some of us were
Afro-Mexican & mentioned our friend
Marcos as an example. He said, "That's
Right. He was Puerto Rican." Actually
He said he was Cuban. We were both wrong.

6.

Our friend Becky has blocked out her memories
Of our elementary where, according
To my childhood friend, she never
Felt welcome. "Because Becky was Black," he
Said. I asked him if she thought of herself
As Black, if he had asked her about it.
He said he had & that she had thought to
Herself for a second before saying
"Yeah." Mexican is not a race either.
Even when Rob Wilson would get angry
& call my childhood friend Messcan
Even when he told me he liked me but
Couldn't date Mexicans, Mexican was
Not a race—not even in the 80s.

7.

Where am I going with this? I thought
I knew. It makes sense that whenever race
Comes up, I think about the Rio Grande
Valley—"the Valley" as anyone
Who knows the place calls it. That's where I learned
I'm not white & what that means & how what
That means changes & doesn't & to who.
Harlingen (where I was born & raised) is
The whitest town in the Valley. Anglos
Made up about 10% of the town
When I lived there. My extended family
Lived in Brownsville & La Joya. Anglos
Made & make up less than 7%
Of both of those towns. Where is this going?

8.

Gloria Anzaldúa was also
From the Valley. Her Wikipedia
Page says she was born in Harlingen like
Me. I read *Borderlands/La Frontera:*
The New Mestiza in college, after
One of my Philosophy professors
Recommended it to me. At the time
I was more than anything excited
To be from the same place as this published
Writer, but to be honest, I didn't
Understand how "living between cultures"
Made us special. I didn't even see
How the "cultures" were distinct. I still don't.
Her approach didn't resonate with me.

.

9.

Anzaldúa died from complications
Associated with diabetes
In 2004. She was 61.
Around the same age as my Aunt Licha
Who also died from complications
Associated with diabetes
Around that time. Imagining these two
Women—one in Santa Cruz, the other
In Harlingen—dying, it's hard not to
Reflect on what I know about their lives.
How different they were. My aunt loved reading
Too, but the *Bible*. Her approach didn't
Resonate with me either, but my love
Of reading was always compared to hers.

10.

My dad would always say we were people
Of the mud—Native, Spanish, mud. My mom
Would say, "No seas Malinche," sometimes.
I always thought that was a thing, rather
Than a person you could be, then later
After reading Anzaldúa, I thought
One day I would write about Malinche.
After Anzaldúa, who insisted
The demise of the Aztec Empire
Wasn't one woman's fault, who understood
That the Aztec's treatment of other tribes
Contributed to their own destruction
As it subverted solidarity
Among Natives against the Spanish. Yeah.

.

11.

Looking at the story of Malinche
Only got me so far. *Genesis* by
Eduardo Galeano, the first book
In his *Memory of Fire*, got me
Farther. *Black in Latin America*
With Henry Louis Gates, Jr. did, too.
How do enslaved Africans fit into
The story of Malinche? Where were they?
That story became more interesting
More important to me than Malinche's.
In the Americas, only Brazil
Had more African slaves than New Spain. From
The time of Cortés to the election
Of Guerrero, there were African slaves.
.
.

12.

Mestizaje refers to the general
Process of mixing ancestries. Some say
As an ideology it's kind of
"An alibi for the nation"—tied to
Nationalist interests, it celebrates
Racial diversity even as it
Denies the hierarchies race stems from—
As real as they are divisive. It has
Circulated in the Caribbean
& in Hispanic America—"most
Notoriously in Brazil"—though now
In decline. In Mexico, the goal under
This ideology was the homo-
Genization of all ethnicities.

13.

When I say "the homogenization
Of all ethnicities" I mean the goal
Was to erase Black Mexicans. José
Vasconcelos's essay "La Raza
Cósmica" begins with him explaining
How he thinks the human races evolved
& it only gets worse as he goes on.
He sounds like a Nazi as he lays out
A hierarchy of races with Black
At the bottom & white at the top, though
He imagines a mixed race, a new shade
Of white, that will trump them all. He sounds like
A Nazi who believes "the Indian's
A good bridge" between the Black race & white.

14.

Vasconcelos believed "the Indians"
Did or would eventually see themselves
As Mexican first—even after he
Laid out that hierarchy of races
He believed that. You can share a country
Like you can share a culture—with people
Who want you to disappear, who would take
Everything from you & still want you gone
Who would ask that you stand by silently
Or actively help as they make others
Disappear & all involved might enjoy
Dancing to "La Bamba" & not even
Know it was originally a song
Sung by African slaves in Veracruz.

15.

The story of Malinche always seemed
Sexist to me so its anti-blackness
Isn't that surprising, but beyond that
Story, there are others I share with those
Of Mexican &/or Latin descent
The mere mention of which will remind me
Of how I felt when I found out César
Chávez was no friend to people
He called "wetbacks," will remind me of all
The Latinos working for the Border
Patrol & Immigration & Customs
Enforcement (ICE), will remind me of how
Vasconcelos describes the white race as
One split into Anglos & Latinos.

16.

A border, like race, is a cruel fiction
Maintained by constant policing, violence
Always threatening a new map. It takes
Time, lots of people's time, to organize
The world this way. & violence. It takes more
Violence. Violence no one can confuse for
Anything but violence. So much violence
Changes relationships, births a people
They can reason with. These people are not
Us. They underestimate the violence.
It's been a while. We are who we are
To them, even when we don't know who we
Are to each other & culture is a
Record of us figuring that out.

17.

Why didn't Anzaldúa write about
The Plan of San Diego? She mentions
"Mexican-American resisters"
robbed a train in Brownsville in October
1915 & the brutality
Of white vigilante groups & Texas
Rangers that followed, but she says nothing
Of the Plan, its appeal to all factions
Of the Mexican Revolution to
Cooperate in a struggle against
The United States, the way it echoed
Writings in Ricardo Flores Magón's
Newspaper *Regeneración*, which had
Its share of subscribers in the Valley.

18.

One of those subscribers—Aniceto
Pizaña wrote a 21-verse poem
About leaving San Benito after
Suffering anti-Mexican abuse.
He says, "With suffering and pain that grows
Greater / I say that there are Mexicans
Who hate and despise their own race…to lick
The feet of the Americans." It's hard
To say who precisely Pizaña is
Referring to when he says "Mexicans"
& there's the familiar conflation of
Nationality & race, but the lack
Of solidarity among people
Of Mexican descent against Anglos…

19.

It's still like that. Pizaña moved away
from San Benito, in any case
& settled in Brownsville, where he did find
Like-minded people, who also subscribed
To *Regeneración*—like Emilia
Rodriguez, a widow who supported
Herself as a seamstress & took part in
A women's discussion group. She might have
Especially appreciated the September
3rd issue in 1910, its front page
Coverage of both "ethnic exclusion
Of Mexicans by whites" in Texas &
Mujer Moderna's editor living
In exile in San Antonio.

20.

According to passengers who survived
The attack & robbery of the train
Anzaldúa mentions in *Borderlands*
The "resisters'" chants included "Viva
Aniceto Pizaña!" It makes sense.
A posse of Anglos that included
Texas Rangers & other officials
Had raided his ranch just two months
Before. Pizaña & some of his friends
Shot & killed one of the men & wounded
Three others in the process then escaped.
Pizaña later claimed the raid drove him
To join the Plan of San Diego, though
He'd been the Anglos' nightmare long before.

21.

Lots of people don't talk about the Plan
Of San Diego. Take back Texas, New
Mexico, Arizona, Wyoming
& California; annex six more states
For an independent republic of
Black people; return to the Apaches
Their land; kill all white American males
Over the age of 16. That's the Plan.
To some people it just doesn't sound real
But I agree with the historian
Gerald Horne: even "if the 'Plan' was a
Fiction, massacres of various sorts
Were not," neither was the temporary
Halt of economic development.

22.

1915-1917
The Valley was "a virtual war zone."
Whether that was the Plan or only looked
Like part of the Plan, the effects reached well
Beyond the Valley, in part, because some
Feared Germany & Japan were behind
It. But Black militancy, on the rise
At the time, "gave the Plan resonance &
Terrified Washington." It wasn't just
That Afro-Mexicans & African-
Americans living in the US
Might join the movement. They feared mutiny.
They feared Black soldiers, who were typically
Stationed in the borderlands around that time.

23.

No one remembers the Alamo or
Vicente Guerrero or the ban on
Communication between Mexicans
& slaves in parts of Texas. I don't know
How much it matters, but I imagine
A Valley where you learn about the Plan
Growing up & the "Buffalo Soldiers"
Of the 24th infantry, who marched
On Jim Crow Houston's predominantly
Black San Felipe district & opened
Fire on the police—I imagine
Life in that Valley & how it would be
Harder to not hear these stories in that
Place. It's hard to imagine but I try.

24.

Vasconcelos opened a law office
To support himself in San Diego
California, the same year Black soldiers
Killed cops in Houston. He'd spent quite a bit
Of time in the US by then — even
Before exile. Didier Jaén says
"He lived the Chicano experience"
When his dad was a Customs Inspector
In Piedras Negras & he was going
To school in Eagle Pass. Jaén believes this
Explains, at least in part, why Chicanos
Saw "La Raza" in his "Cosmic race" when
The concept had already fallen out
Of favor in Latin America.

25.

Since I started writing this poem less than
A year ago, Mexico recognized
The African ancestry of more than
1 million Mexicans for the first time
In a census survey. "Black" will debut
As an official category in
The 2020 national census.
This is decades after the much discussed
"Multicultural turn" of the 90s
In Latin America, when people
Of African descent went from being
"Invisible" to becoming part of
The state's apparatus, "communities"
Lawyers could find a legal way around.

26.

In the US, the 2000 census
Allowed respondents to check all races
That applied. It was either that or add
A "multiracial" category. It
Was the choice that split the Multiracial
Movement. The middle class white women who
Started the Movement were on the same side
Of the debate as Newt Gingrich, wanting
A standalone category that would
Have affected the numbers of other
Minority racial categories
& funding for race-based initiatives
& civil rights programs. Their primary
Concern was their children's "racial safety."

27.

When I say the middle class white women
Who started the Multiracial Movement
Were concerned about their children's "racial
Safety," I mean they could see their children
Weren't white, but they wanted everyone else
To see how they weren't Black either—cuz "safety."
Groups like the NAACP did
Not like them. The white women didn't get
It. They thought these groups must be for the "one-
Drop rule." In his book *Amalgamation
Schemes*, Jared Sexton attacks the Movement
& celebrations of "impurity"
In general—Anzaldúa's included.
"Impurity's" a given. Race is not.

28.

What gets me: the Multiracial Movement
Started in San Francisco in 19-
78, when "urban renewal"
Was displacing thousands of Black people.
The white women who started it had to
Have known. '78 was the same year
Many of the Fillmore District's former
Black residents committed suicide
Or were murdered in Jonestown, Guyana.
That had to have been all over the news.
But there's no indication these women
Wanted to fight that kind of racism.
Vasconcelos's case is more complex
Not cuz he was mestizo. He was not.

29.

I keep thinking of this woman I met
At a "POC only" meeting years
Ago. She wasn't just light-skinned. She looked
White. It's hard to explain, but I wasn't
Alone in thinking this. When it was her
Turn, she introduced herself & explained
Her father was white & her mother was
From Guatemala. She offered to leave
If anyone was uncomfortable
With her there. Everyone said it was fine.
Only later did I learn from a friend
Who'd dated her & met her mother, her
Mother's family owned a plantation in
Guatemala. Otherwise they were Basque.

30.

The Magón brothers founded the Eden-
Dale commune with family & friends in Los
Angeles, surrounded by silent film
Studios in Silver Lake. There has to
Be room for that. That & everything else
That was un-American at that time
In the broadest, anti-capitalist
Sense. A friend once said race is what is done
To us; ethnicity is what we do
To ourselves. Growing up in the Valley
That didn't feel true, but that doesn't mean
It isn't. Even in 1915
Trains travelling through Brownsville segregated
Black people from white. Mexican or not.

ACKNOWLEDGMENTS

Many thanks to the editors of the following print & online publications, where some of these poems first appeared: *West Wind Review, Armed Cell, With+Stand, LIES Journal, The American Reader, OMG!, Tripwire, Hi Zero, Scream Queens, Hold: a Journal, Aspasiology, The Elephants, & Social Text.*

I would also like to thank the organizers of the Poetic Labor Project where I first presented "The We of a Position." That day in Oakland, in the early fall of 2011, remains very important to me.

To Dana Ward & Paul Coors at Perfect Lovers Press, who published my first chapbook *128-131*, and to Jocelyn Saidenberg, Stephanie Young & Brandon Brown at Krupskaya Books who held my hand through the publication of *Narrative*, your early & ongoing encouragement has been critical to the work collected here. Thank you.

& to the editors of Commune Editions — Jasper Bernes, Joshua Clover, & Juliana Spahr — thank you not only for your encouragement & constant engagement of my work, but also for wanting more than poetry & being loud & clear about it. If over the last decade there hadn't been more than poetry, this book wouldn't exist. Of course, it's probably also true that this book wouldn't exist if over the last decade things had gone as we wanted. Whatever. I'm glad that together we've been a small part of more than poetry.

Finally & not unrelated to the vast majority of people I've already thanked, I want to thank my comrades. Even if I was to limit it to those whose (not necessarily real) names I know, there'd be too many to list here. For that, too, I'm thankful. It wasn't always like this.